GEORGIA LAW REQUIRES LIBRARY
MATERIALS TO BE RETURNED OR
REPLACEMENT COSTS PAID.
(O.C.G.A. 20-5-53)

PEACHTREE CITY
PLAN TO STAY™

PEACHTREE CITY LIBRARY
201 Willowbend Road
Peachtree City, GA 30269-1623
Phone: 770-631-2520
Fax: 770-631-2522

George S. Patton Jr.

History Maker Bios

Jane Sutcliffe

LERNER PUBLICATIONS COMPANY • MINNEAPOLIS

For those who were lucky enough to say, "I fought with Patton"

Map on p. 38 by Laura Westlund
Illustrations by Tim Parlin

Text copyright © 2005 by Jane Sutcliffe
Illustrations copyright © 2005 by Lerner Publishing Group, Inc.

Lerner Publications Company
A division of Lerner Publishing Group, Inc.
241 First Avenue North
Minneapolis, MN 55401 U.S.A.

Website address: www.lernerbooks.com

Library of Congress Cataloging-in-Publication Data

Sutcliffe, Jane.
    George S. Patton Jr. / by Jane Sutcliffe.
      p.   cm. — (History maker bios)
    Includes bibliographical references and index.
    ISBN-13: 978–0–8225–2436–6 (lib. bdg. : alk. paper)
    ISBN-10: 0–8225–2436–8 (lib. bdg. : alk. paper)
      1. Patton, George S. (George Smith), 1885–1945—Juvenile literature.
    2. Generals—United States—Biography—Juvenile literature. 3. United States.
    Army—Biography—Juvenile literature. 4. United States—History, Military—
    20th century—Juvenile literature. I. Title. II. Series.
    E745.P3S87 2005
    355'.0092—dc22   2004002590

Manufactured in the United States of America
2 3 4 5 6 7 – SS – 13 12 11 10 09 08

TABLE OF CONTENTS

INTRODUCTION

George S. Patton Jr. always wanted to be a soldier. He dreamed of leading a great army in battle. He got his chance when he led U.S. soldiers through two world wars. Together, he and his men chased the enemy and fought in fierce combat. He never lost a battle.

George became one of the greatest generals in U.S. history. His soldiers were proud of him. The American people cheered for him. And the enemy feared him.

This is his story.

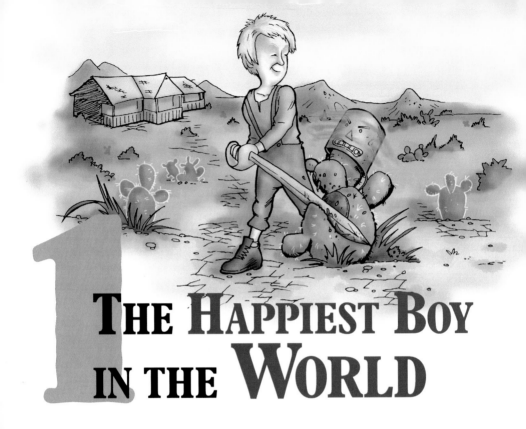

1 THE HAPPIEST BOY IN THE WORLD

He was "Georgie S. Patton Jr., Lieutenant General." At least, that's what he liked to call himself. From the time he was seven years old, George Patton knew just what he wanted to be.

George was born on November 11, 1885. He was the only son of Ruth and George S. Patton II, so his parents called him simply, "the boy." George also had a younger sister Anne. Everyone called her "Nita."

George and Nita grew up on their family's big ranch in San Gabriel, California. George wasn't the kind of boy to just sit around. He played with his dogs and rode his horses. His father—George called him Papa—taught him how to fish and sail and shoot a rifle. George called himself "the happiest boy in the world."

Every night, George climbed onto Papa's lap. He listened as Papa read to him. Papa's books were full of thrilling stories about brave soldiers, great generals, and the battles they fought.

George, age ten, with his mother and sister

Some of the stories Papa told were about George's relatives. George's great-great-great-grandfather had fought with George Washington in the American Revolution. His grandfather had been a Confederate soldier—and a hero—in the Civil War.

George listened to these stories again and again. He thought that being a soldier sounded wonderful. He liked to pretend that he was a soldier too. He had a little soldier suit with a tall, fancy hat. Once Papa gave him a real sword. George used it to whack away at a cactus plant.

George's grandfather (LEFT) was an officer in the Confederate army during the Civil War.

WHY COULDN'T GEORGE READ?

George had a reading disorder called dyslexia (dis-LEK-see-uh). Like others with this disorder, George struggled with reading, writing, and spelling. Once he joked, "Any idiot can spell a word the same way time after time. But it calls for imagination . . . to be able to spell it several different ways as I do."

For a long time, Papa's books were George's only schooling. George was a bright boy. But he didn't learn to read when other children did. Somehow, the words on a page just didn't make sense to him.

Mama and Papa were afraid that other schoolchildren would tease George, so they didn't send him to school. Instead, Papa read to him. Private teachers helped too. George didn't go to a real school until he was nearly twelve.

George spent his time enjoying the outdoors during his summers at Catalina Island.

The Pattons spent every summer on Catalina Island, off the coast of California. In the summer of 1902, when George was sixteen, he met a girl named Beatrice Ayer. Her family was spending the summer there too.

Beatrice was pretty and smart. Best of all, she liked the same things George did. The two spent the summer riding horses, swimming, and sailing. By the end of the summer, George and Beatrice were in love. They promised to write to each other.

George had never stopped thinking about becoming a soldier. In June 1904, he entered the U.S. Army's college for soldiers. It was in West Point, New York.

More than anything, George wanted to do well at West Point. He spent many hours studying. Sometimes he got up before dawn to study more. It was hard to watch other students study less and get better grades.

George learned to be a soldier while he attended West Point.

In the end, George failed one of his classes. He had to repeat the year.

George did not intend to fail again. In fact, he did not intend to fail at *anything.* He studied harder than ever. In football, he played so hard that he broke his arm— twice. He learned to fight with a sword, a sport called fencing. Quickly, he became one of the best in the class.

George became an expert at fencing. He later wrote this U.S. Army manual about fencing.

WAR DEPARTMENT : OFFICE OF THE CHIEF OF STAFF

Saber Exercise

1914

WASHINGTON
GOVERNMENT PRINTING OFFICE
1914

Above all, George was determined to look and act like the perfect soldier. When the students had to stand at attention, no one stood straighter than George. In his last year, he was named second in command of all the students. It was his job to read out orders from the center of the parade ground. He liked the attention.

In June 1909, when he was twenty-three, George graduated from West Point. Papa watched proudly as Mama and Beatrice pinned the gold bars of an army officer on him. At last, George was a real soldier.

2 First Battle

Blood flowed down George's face. He had been training young soldiers at Fort Sheridan, Illinois. Suddenly, his horse threw its head back, cutting George's forehead. It was a painful wound. But George calmly continued the drill. The men were amazed at their officer's toughness.

George enjoyed his duties at Fort Sheridan. Only one thing was missing— Beatrice Ayer. She and George were more in love than ever. On May 26, 1910, they were married. They settled into army life.

In 1911, Lieutenant George Patton was transferred to Fort Myer in Washington, D.C. There, he got exciting news. The army had chosen him to take part in the 1912 Olympic Games in Stockholm, Sweden. He would compete in a new event, open only to soldiers. The event was really five sports in one. George would have to run, swim, shoot, ride a horse, and fence.

George and Beatrice married on May 26, 1910.

At the Olympics, George attacked each event as if it were a battle. He swam so hard he had to be pulled out of the pool with a hook. He fainted after his footrace. George came in fifth overall. He probably wasn't happy about it, but he made no excuses. Instead, he just wanted to work harder. He especially wanted to work on his fencing. He studied with the best swordsman in Europe. Soon he was an expert himself.

George created his own type of fencing sword (RIGHT).

The army made him a teacher and gave him the fancy title "Master of the Sword." He even designed a new kind of blade. Before long, soldiers all over the country were carrying the "Patton sword."

George was pleased with his accomplishments, but what he truly wanted was a real battle. In September 1915, he was sent to Fort Bliss in Texas. While he was there, Mexican raiders attacked the town of Columbus, New Mexico. Eighteen Americans died.

The camp at Fort Bliss, 1915

The army was ordered to capture the raiders. George was excited about the chance to fight. But then came bad news. He was not going.

George was not about to miss his big chance. He boldly asked the commanding general if he could go along. "Everyone wants to go," the general pointed out. "Why should I favor you?"

A New George

George didn't think he looked much like a soldier. So he decided to change. He practiced making a fierce-looking scowl in the mirror. He called it his war face. He learned to curse too. Most people thought that this rough and tough George was the real George S. Patton. They didn't know that this was just George's idea of how a soldier should act.

U.S. soldiers stand guard over captured raiders who were part of the attack on Columbus, New Mexico, in 1915.

"Because I want to go more than anyone else," George answered. The general agreed to take George along as his assistant.

Some of George's duties were boring. He took notes for the general and went on errands. But there was always a chance for a fight.

Once he was sent to a farm to buy corn. On the way back, George stopped at a nearby ranch. He had a hunch that one of the head raiders might be hiding there.

George and other soldiers were riding in three cars. He ordered the cars to surround the house. Then he started toward the gate that led to the courtyard. Suddenly, three men on horseback charged out of the gate. They were shooting at George and his men. George fired back. So did the soldiers with him.

The courtyard thundered with the crack of gunfire. When the last echo had died away, all three horsemen were dead. One of them was the raider.

The story of the shootout appeared in newspapers across the country. It was the first time that automobiles were used in battle. Until then, soldiers had used horses. George had started a whole new kind of combat.

George was pleased. He wrote to Beatrice, "I have at last succeeded in getting into a fight."

There was an even bigger fight to come.

3 A BIG CHANCE

George returned from Mexico in February 1917. But he had no time to rest. Two months later, the United States entered World War I. Soon, George was on his way to Europe to fight in the war.

Soldiers in Europe were using a new invention called a tank. These machines crawled over the ground on metal belts. They could plow through thick brush or climb over rocks.

George was in charge
of an army tank school
in France in 1918.

George was fascinated by tanks. He
applied for the U.S. Army's new tank corps.
He reminded the general in charge, "I am
the only American who has ever made an
attack in a motor vehicle."

Perhaps that's what did the trick. Not
only was George accepted but he was also
picked to run the army's new tank school.

First, George went to a tank center in
France. He learned everything he could
about tanks. Then, in February 1918, he met
his first students.

George was both a teacher and the boss. He also had to be a bit like a coach. He was training his soldiers not for a game, but for battle. He was tough on his men. Some of the men grumbled about all of George's rules. But they liked being on his team.

By late summer, George had 950 men in his school. He wasn't just their teacher. He was also the man who would lead them on the battlefield. It would be the first time that U.S. tanks were used in a war. "This is our big chance," he told his men, "what we have worked for."

ALWAYS A SOLDIER

George believed he had lived as a soldier in past lives. In one life, for example, he was a soldier in ancient Rome. In another, he sailed with the Vikings.

Some people smiled at George's idea of past lives. But George liked thinking that, even after he died, he'd be a soldier again someday.

Their first fight was near the town of Saint-Mihiel, France. Before the battle, George gave his soldiers an important order. He told them to keep moving forward, no matter what. George led by example. Once, during a battle, he saw five tanks waiting at a bridge. The drivers were afraid to cross. They had heard that bombs were attached to the bridge. George didn't know if there were bombs or not. Still, he walked across the bridge as the tanks followed.

U.S. soldiers in tanks move forward through France during World War I.

U.S. soldiers in battle in the Argonne Forest in 1918

Two weeks later, George and his soldiers attacked an area between the Meuse River and the Argonne Forest. During the battle, he came across some soldiers who wanted to run away. George shouted and cursed at them to keep them from retreating.

He led the men up and over a hill. Suddenly, the enemy began firing at them. George and his men dropped to the ground. He knew that they should be moving forward. But he was too afraid.

Then George looked up. The clouds in the sky looked like faces to him. He imagined his relatives who had died in battle. George couldn't disappoint them. He got up and faced the bullets. He knew he could be killed.

He nearly was. A bullet tore through his leg. He lost a lot of blood. Another man dragged him into a ditch and stopped the bleeding.

George's tanks went on to help win the battle. But for George, the fighting was over. He spent the next month in a hospital.

He was still getting better when he learned that the war was over. The United States and its allies had won. It was November 11, 1918—George's thirty-third birthday.

4 A NICE JUICY WAR

Most people would have thought that world peace was a wonderful birthday present. Not George. He missed the war.

Once, after returning home, he went to a play about the war. The play was full of exciting sound effects—booming cannons and banging guns. But the noise just made George miss war even more.

George continued working for the army, helping officers and staying in the background. But George didn't like the background. He liked being in the spotlight. He wanted to lead soldiers in battle again.

In September 1939, World War II began in Europe. U.S. soldiers weren't in the war yet. Still, the army wanted to be ready. George was sent to Fort Benning, Georgia, to train soldiers. After twenty years, he was commanding tanks again.

The United States started building tanks in early 1940 to be prepared in case of war.

OLD BLOOD AND GUTS

George once told his men that wars were won with "blood and guts." Somebody thought that would make a good nickname. Before long, everybody was calling George "Old Blood and Guts"—though not to his face.

George didn't like what he saw in his new soldiers. He thought they were sloppy. So he gave new orders. His men were to dress neatly, with shoes shined and hair trimmed.

George's soldiers learned to do whatever it took to win a battle. Once they took part in a huge practice battle. They drove their tanks on roads throughout the South. The tanks ran out of gas. George used his own money to buy fuel at gas stations. Other commanders complained that this was against the rules. There were no rules in war, George reminded them.

The United States entered World War II after Pearl Harbor was bombed by the Japanese.

Newspaper reporters loved George's colorful ways. They wrote stories about him. Soon the whole country knew George's name. At last, he had the spotlight right where he wanted it.

George's training paid off. His soldiers were ready to fight. All they needed was what George called a "nice juicy war."

He got one. In December 1941, the United States entered the war against Germany, Japan, and Italy. The army and the American public expected great things from George. He did not disappoint them.

In their first battle in North Africa, U.S. troops were beaten badly. Some of the soldiers had panicked. They ran away. People were saying that U.S. soldiers did not have the nerve to fight.

George stepped in. In only ten days, he turned the defeated soldiers into a spirited fighting unit. When the next battle came, they fought hard and won.

In North Africa, Patton leads U.S. troops to victory.

In Sicily, Italy, George was ordered to capture the town of Messina. His soldiers and British soldiers would march to Messina by separate roads. Then they would capture the town together.

But George was sure that the British troops would grab all the glory. He turned the march into a race. George won his race with only an hour to spare. Even the British soldiers were impressed. One of them shook George's hand and told him it was a "jolly good race."

Patton's troops enter Messina, Sicily, Italy, in 1943.

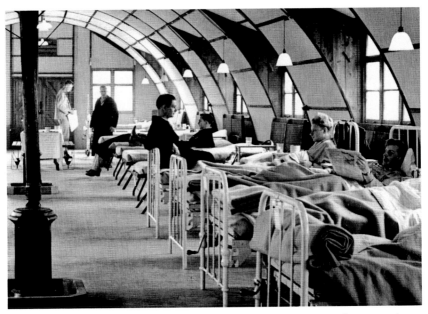

Sick and wounded soldiers recover in an army hospital during World War II.

Often, George went to hospitals to visit wounded soldiers. He praised them and pinned medals on them. Sometimes he cried with them.

Once he came across a soldier with no bandages. George asked him where he was hurt. The man said he had no wounds. "I guess I just can't take it," he said.

George was angry. He called the soldier a coward. Then he took his gloves and slapped the man across the face.

A week later, the same thing happened. This time, he threatened to shoot the soldier for being a coward. He even waved his pistol in the air.

Doctors and nurses were shocked. They wrote a letter to George's commander, General Dwight Eisenhower, who was also horrified. He could have kicked George out of the army for slapping soldiers.

George was ordered to apologize to the men. He also had to apologize to the doctors and nurses, as well as to all the men under his command. George did as he was told.

When he tried to apologize to his men, though, they wouldn't listen. Instead, they began to cheer. They wouldn't let him finish what he had come to say.

5 PATTON, OF COURSE

The army needed George. The United States and its allies had a new plan. They were going to smash the German army once and for all. They would need George to help them do it.

On June 6, 1944, soldiers landed on the beaches of Normandy, France. They fought German soldiers there in a fierce and bloody battle.

One month later, George spoke to his men to get them ready for the job ahead. He talked about fighting and about winning. He talked about doing what they had to do—even when they were scared. His words sparked with energy.

The men cheered. He "makes you feel like you can do anything and nothing can stop you," one soldier said.

Patton directs his troops in Europe in 1944.

LISTENING TO GEORGE

George was famous for the speeches he gave his men. But most people were surprised when they first heard him. They expected such a great man to have a deep, booming voice. Instead, George's voice was high-pitched and squeaky.

The idea was for the soldiers to drive their tanks across France. They would push the enemy back. Moving ahead, no matter what, was what George did best. At once, his tanks rolled forward. His men raced across the French countryside. German soldiers ran. Thousands of them gave up.

By the end of August, George's tanks were close to Germany. If he could keep going, he could defeat the Germans.

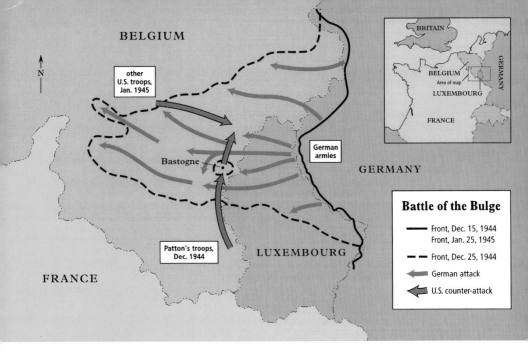

Battle of the Bulge, December 1944

Before they reached Germany, the tanks began to sputter. One by one, they stopped. They were out of fuel.

It was nearly winter before George was able to get gas again. That was just long enough for the enemy to grow stronger. They were ready to fight back.

On December 16, the German army struck. German soldiers came through a forest in Belgium. On a map, the battleground had a bulging shape, so the battle became known as the Battle of the Bulge.

The attack took U.S. soldiers by surprise. Thousands were killed. Many more were trapped in the town of Bastogne. They were surrounded.

On December 19, Eisenhower held a meeting. He needed someone to speed north to drive the enemy back. He turned to George. "When can you attack?" he asked.

"On December 22," George answered.

Only three days away! The others in the room laughed. They thought George was just boasting. But George meant what he said. He got his soldiers moving right away. The weather was terrible. The roads were icy and covered with snow. But George was ready, just as he'd promised.

Troops march through cold winter conditions.

For four days, his men fought the enemy soldiers surrounding Bastogne. Finally, they broke through. They swept into the town to help the soldiers there.

George was headline news again. One reporter wrote that he always seemed to be the one who came to the rescue. The headline at the top of the article read: "PATTON OF COURSE."

U.S. soldiers fire on German troops outside of Bastogne.

Patton rides in a parade in Los Angeles, California, in 1945. The crowd celebrates his many victories in World War II.

The battle was the beginning of the end for the German soldiers. Within three weeks, their big attack had failed. Then, in May 1945, Germany surrendered. The United States and its allies had won.

George was welcomed back to the United States with parades and fireworks. He rode through the streets as thousands cheered. They wanted to see the hero they had read so much about.

George with his wife and children in the early 1930s

But there was still work to do in Europe. In July, George went back. Except for a month at home, he had been away from his family for more than two and a half years.

George planned to go home again later that year. He was due to leave on December 10. On December 9, he and some friends were riding in the back of a car. Suddenly, a truck swerved toward them. It crashed into the car.

George was the only one hurt in the crash. He hit his head and injured his spinal cord. He couldn't move at all. At the hospital, a doctor told him the sad news: he would never walk or ride a horse again.

On December 21, 1945, George died. He was sixty years old. He was buried in a cemetery in Europe. Five thousand other U.S. soldiers were buried there too. All of them had fought with George. They would have been proud to have him with them.

Patton's headstone is marked with the date of his death, December 21, 1945.

TIMELINE

GEORGE S. PATTON JR.
WAS BORN ON
NOVEMBER 11, 1885.

In the year . . .

1909	George graduated from West Point in June.	Age 23
	he became an officer at Fort Sheridan, Illinois, in September.	
1910	he married Beatrice Ayer.	
1911	he was transferred to Fort Myer in Washington, D.C.	
1912	he competed in the Olympic Games in Stockholm, Sweden.	Age 26
1914	World War I began in Europe.	
1916	he joined the army expedition to Mexico.	
1917	the United States entered World War I.	
1918	he started a school for tank soldiers in February.	Age 32
	he led men in battle in September.	
1919	he returned to the United States.	
1939	World War II began in Europe.	
1940	he became a commanding officer at Fort Benning, Georgia.	
1941	the United States entered World War II.	
1942–45	he commanded soldiers in North Africa and Europe.	
1945	World War II ended in Europe in May.	Age 60
	he died on December 21.	

"THAT WAS PATTON"

Not all of George's soldiers liked him. Some thought he was a bigmouth and a bully. But most stood tall when they said they had fought with George S. Patton Jr.

The day after George's death, one of his soldiers wrote home to his parents: "Last night one of the greatest men that ever lived died. That was Patton. The rest of the world thinks of him as just another guy with stars on his shoulders. The men that served under him know him as a soldier's leader. I am proud to say that I have served under him. . . . "

Further Reading

Cornish, Geoff. *Tanks.* **Minneapolis: Lerner Publications Company, 2004.** Profiles some of the different tanks and other armored fighting vehicles used by armies around the world.

Hughes, Dean. *Soldier Boys.* **New York: Atheneum Books for Young Readers, 2001.** The fictional story of two boys, one German and one American, who are eager to join their respective armies during World War II. Their paths cross at the Battle of the Bulge.

McNeese, Tim. *Battle of the Bulge.* **Philadelphia: Chelsea House Publishers, 2004.** Recounts events leading up to and surrounding the 1944–45 Battle of the Bulge in Ardennes, France, during World War II.

Rice, Earle, Jr. *George S. Patton.* **Philadelphia: Chelsea House Publishers, 2004.** Reviews the life and battles of General George S. Patton.

Websites

Patton Museum of Cavalry and Armor
http://www.generalpatton.org
Learn about General Patton and about the Fort Knox museum that preserves old cavalry machines.

Patton Society
http://www.pattonhq.com
Read about General George S. Patton Jr. and learn more about his life at the Patton Society's home page.

SELECT BIBLIOGRAPHY

Blumenson, Martin. *Patton: The Man behind the Legend, 1885–1845.* New York: William Morrow and Company, Inc., 1985.

Blumenson, Martin, ed. *The Patton Papers: 1885–1940.* Boston: Houghton Mifflin Company, 1972.

Blumenson, Martin, ed. *The Patton Papers: 1940–1945.* Boston: Houghton Mifflin Company, 1974.

D'Este, Carlo. *Patton: A Genius for War.* New York: HarperCollins Publishers, 1995.

Devaney, John. *"Blood and Guts": The True Story of Gen. George S. Patton, USA.* New York: Julian Messner, 1982.

Farago, Ladislas. *Patton: Ordeal and Triumph.* New York: Ivan Obolensky, Inc., 1963.

Lande, D. A. *I Was with Patton: First-Person Accounts of WWII in George S. Patton's Command.* Saint Paul: MBI Publishing Company, 2002.

Patton, General George S. *War As I Knew It.* Boston: Houghton Mifflin Company, 1947.

Patton, Robert H. *The Pattons: A Personal History of an American Family.* New York: Crown Publishers, Inc., 1994.

Peifer, Charles, Jr. *Soldier of Destiny: A Biography of George Patton.* Minneapolis: Dillon Press, 1989.

Rice, Earle, Jr. *Strategic Battles in Europe.* San Diego: Lucent Books, Inc., 2000.

INDEX

Acknowledgments

For photographs and artwork: Charles M. Province, The George S. Patton, Jr.
Historical Society. http://www.pattonhq.com Pattonhq@cox.net., pp. 4, 7, 11, 12 (both),
16 (top), 31, 42, 43; Virginia Military Institute Archives, pp. 8, 15; © Lake County
Museum/CORBIS , p. 10; The Patton Museum, p. 16 (bottom); © CORBIS, pp. 17, 36;
© Bettmann/CORBIS, p. 19; National Archives, pp. 22, 24 (W&C 630), 25, 33 (W&C
919), 39 (W&C 1079), 40 (W&C 1074), 41 (W&C 753); Library of Congress, pp. 28 (LC-
USE6-D-001276), 30 (LC-USZ62-16555), 45 (LC-USZ62-25122); © Getty Images, p. 32.
Front cover: © Bettman/CORBIS. **Back cover:** Charles M. Province, The George S.
Patton, Jr. Historical Society. http://www.pattonhq.com Pattonhq@cox.net. Illustrations
by Tim Parlin. Map on page 38 by Laura Westlund.
For quoted material: pp. 7, 20, 22, 23, Martin Blumenson, *The Patton Papers:
1885–1940.* (Boston: Houghton Mifflin Company, 1972); pp. 12, 18, 32, Carlo
D'Este, *Patton: A Genius for War.* (New York: HarperCollins Publishers, 1995);
pp. 30, 40, Robert H. Patton, *The Pattons: A Personal History of an American
Family.* (New York: Crown Publishers, Inc. 1994); pp. 33, 36, D. A. Lande, *I Was
with Patton: First-Person Accounts of WWII in George S. Patton's Command.*
(Saint Paul: MBI Publishing Company, 2002); pp. 39, 45, Martin Blumenson, *The
Patton Papers: 1940–1945.* (Boston: Houghton Mifflin Company, 1974).